CREATURES OF THE NIGHT

BARN OWLS

QUINN M. ARNOLD

CREATIVE EDUCATION • CREATIVE PAPERBACKS

CONTENTS

AS DUSK SETTLES, A BARN OWL PEERS INTO THE DARKNESS. IT TILTS ITS HEAD, LISTENING. THE NIGHT SEEMS SILENT.

BUT THE OWL HEARS SOMETHING. IT TAKES FLIGHT. SWOOPING DOWN INTO A NEARBY FIELD, IT GRABS A VOLE.

BARN OWLS ARE FOUND ON EVERY CONTINENT EXCEPT ANTARCTICA.

Barn owls are **nocturnal**. They live in tree **cavities** or empty buildings near fields. During the day, their brown and white feathers help them blend in with their surroundings. This keeps them safe from hawks, eagles, and other predators.

FACIAL DISC
RIGHT EAR
LEFT EAR

Barn owls have large, dark eyes. In dim light, their eyes glow. They have excellent night vision. Yet barn owls use their hearing to find food.

Heart-shaped faces help barn owls hear. Their feathers form facial discs. These direct sounds to their ears. Barn owl ears are set unevenly on the head. This helps them locate a sound's source.

Long, broad wings and soft, fluffy feathers help owls fly silently. Their prey does not hear them coming. Barn owls eat **rodents**. Sometimes they eat insects and frogs, too. Their sharp **talons** grasp their meal.

BARN OWL DIET

Small prey is swallowed whole. Larger prey is torn apart with the owl's hooked beak. About 12 hours after eating, a barn owl will throw up a **pellet**.

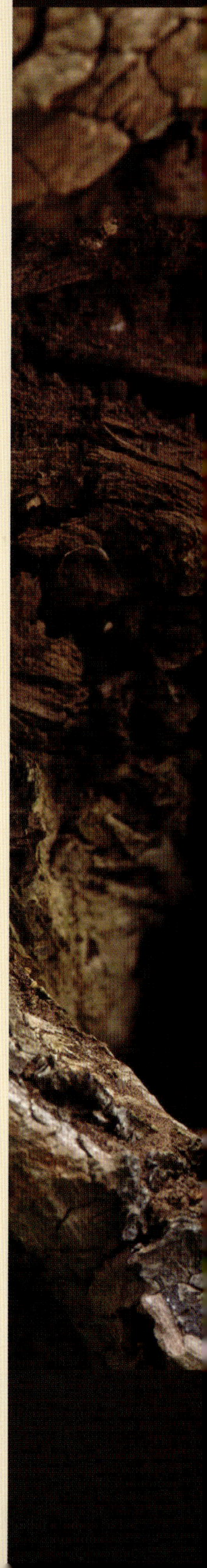

Four to six owlets hatch in a nest. A mother barn owl stays with her babies. She keeps them warm and safe. The father brings food to the nest. Owlets stay with their parents for two or three months.

LIFE OF A BARN OWL

HATCH
breaks out of egg; fluffy white feathers

35–65 DAYS
stiff feathers grow; leaves nest

7–10 WEEKS
begins to fly and hunt

4 MONTHS
parents stop providing food

7 MONTHS
moves away from nest

1 YEAR
finds mate

2 YEARS
end of life

Unlike other owls, barn owls do not hoot. Instead, they screech and hiss. These sounds are often made to scare away threats.

"SCREEEEEEECH!"
"HOO..."

As the sun rises, the barn owl returns to its cavity. It ate well last night and quickly falls asleep. Tucked inside the tree, the owl is warm and safe.

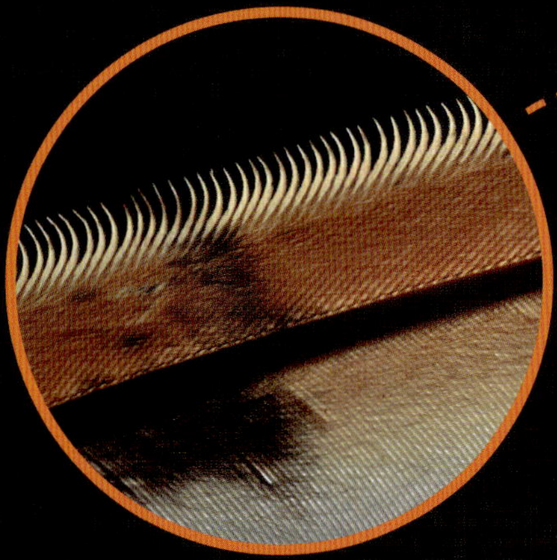

FEATHERS

stiff, comblike edges of wing feathers make flight silent

WINGS

broad and rounded; wingspan can be three times the length of the body

TAIL

short, square-shaped tail helps turn in flight and brake for landing

EYES

large eyes cannot move; owls must rotate and tilt their heads to look around

BEAK

hooked to grip prey and tear apart larger meals

TALONS

sharp and curved to grab prey and grasp branches

GLOSSARY

CAVITIES
empty spaces within a solid object

NOCTURNAL
active at night

PELLET
a small, rounded mass made up of non-digestible parts of prey, such as bones and fur

RODENTS
small mammals with constantly growing front teeth

TALONS
sharp, curved claws

READ MORE

Camisa, Kathryn. *Barn Owl*. New York: Bearport, 2016.

Lynch, Annabelle. *Owls and Owlets*. Mankato, Minn.: Smart Apple Media, 2017.

Marsh, Laura. *Owls*. Washington, D.C.: National Geographic, 2014.

WEBSITES

BioKIDS: Barn Owls
http://www.biokids.umich.edu/critters/Tyto_alba/

Idaho Public Television: Science Trek: Owls
http://idahoptv.org/sciencetrek/topics/owls/index.cfm

NWF: Ranger Rick: Prowl for Owls
https://rangerrick.org/crafts_activities/prowl-for-owls/

Note: Every effort has been made to ensure that the websites listed above are suitable for children, that they have educational value, and that they contain no inappropriate material. However, because of the nature of the Internet, it is impossible to guarantee that these sites will remain active indefinitely or that their contents will not be altered.

INDEX

PUBLISHED BY CREATIVE EDUCATION AND CREATIVE PAPERBACKS

P.O. Box 227, Mankato, Minnesota 56002
Creative Education and Creative Paperbacks are imprints of The Creative Company
www.thecreativecompany.us

LIBRARY OF CONGRESS CATALOGING-IN-PUBLICATION DATA

Names: Arnold, Quinn M., author.
Title: Barn owls / Quinn M. Arnold.
Series: Creatures of the night.
Includes index.
Summary: Peer into the nocturnal forests with this high-interest introduction to the pale, broad-winged birds of prey known as barn owls.

Identifiers:
LCCN: 2018059116
ISBN 978-1-64026-117-4 (hardcover)
ISBN 978-1-62832-680-2 (pbk)
ISBN 978-1-64000-235-7 (eBook)

Subjects: LCSH: Barn owl—Juvenile literature.
Nocturnal animals—Juvenile literature.
Classification: LCC QL696.S85 A76 2019 / DDC 598.9/7—dc23

CCSS: RI.1.1-6; RI.2.1-7; RF.1.1-4; RF.2.1-4

DESIGN AND PRODUCTION

by Joe Kahnke; art direction by Rita Marshall
Printed in China

PHOTOGRAPHS by Alamy (andy aughey, Avalon/Photoshot License, Paul Bolotov, Jenna Chamberlain, Fotoflair Animals, Edo Schmidt), Getty Images (Michael Duva/Stone, Frank Greenaway/Dorling Kindersley, Joel Sartore, National Geographic Photo Ark/National Geographic Images Collection), iStockphoto (DepthofField, LueratSatichob), Minden Pictures (Jose Luis GOMEZ de FRANCISCO/NPL, Paul Sawer/FLPA), Shutterstock (k009034, Stephen Clarke, Eric Isselee, Stephen Marques, MZPHOTO.CZ, NadzeyaShanchuk, Alex Ramsay, Bahruz Rzayev, Dirk Wegman)

FIRST EDITION HC 9 8 7 6 5 4 3 2 1
FIRST EDITION PBK 9 8 7 6 5 4 3 2 1